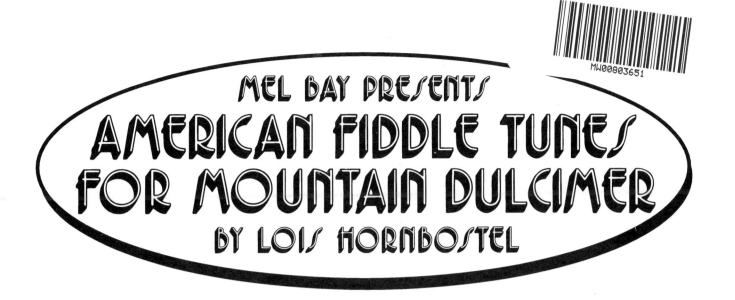

MEL BAY PRESENTS
AMERICAN FIDDLE TUNES
FOR MOUNTAIN DULCIMER
BY LOIS HORNBOSTEL

Arranged for the novice to experienced player in traditional keys, with musical notation
so the selections can be played with other instruments. Accompaniment chords included.

SPECIAL APPRECIATION goes to the gifted musicians who over the centuries have created and contributed to our traditional American fiddle tunes. Lois wishes to thank her musical partners and teachers, among them Jerry Rockwell, Jeff and Janet Furman, Ray Owens, Kenneth Bloom, Jacob Ray Melton, Wayne Seymour, Bill Taylor, Bill Spencer, Ralph Lee Smith, Bill McCloud, Sally George, and Charles Hornbostel, Jr. Special thanks go to William Bay for his encouragement and support on this project.

The mountain dulcimer on this book's cover was handmade for it
by Bill Taylor, Taylor Made Dulcimers, Pigeon Forge, Tennessee.

Visit us on the Web at http://www.melbay.com — E-mail us at email@melbay.com

Sweet Sunny South & Lois — Galax Fiddlers Convention, July 1985.
Top row, left to right: Ted Currin, Tim Currin, and Fred Reynolds. Bottom row, left to right: Wayne Seymour and Lois Hornbostel.

CONTENTS

ALPHABETICAL LISTING OF TUNES

OTHER MOUNTAIN DULCIMER BOOKS & RECORDINGS BY LOIS HORNBOSTEL

DULCIMER FIDDLE TUNES (MB93713) book & recording

ANTHOLOGY FOR THE FRETTED DULCIMER (MB93850) book

THE IRISH DULCIMER (MB93661) book

DULCIMER DUETS, ROUNDS & ENSEMBLES (MB94041) book & recording

THE CLASSROOM DULCIMER (Backyard Music, P.O. Box 9047, New Haven, CT 06532-0047) beginner's book

DULCIMER ENCHANTMENT (Lois Hornbostel, c/o Mel Bay Publications, Inc.) recording containing several selections from above Mel Bay books

INTRODUCTION

Dear Dulcimer Friends,

It seems only a short time since Mel Bay published my first book of fiddle tunes for mountain dulcimer in 1981. DULCIMER FIDDLE TUNES (MB93713) and its companion recording are still very available and are a good prelude to this book. In the years since 1981, I have been thrilled to meet new dulcimer friends from all over the U.S. and other countries who play beautifully the arrangements from DULCIMER FIDDLE TUNES. They play them in jam sessions, have won dulcimer competitions with them, have adapted them to their own styles for performance and recordings, and have also taught me new ways of interpreting the tunes.

Over these years I have learned many new fiddle tunes and approaches to playing them on the mountain dulcimer. My musical roads have happily taken me to fiddle conventions like those in Galax, VA, Fiddlers Grove, NC, and Dublin, VA, where I have grown even closer to this music and have been fortunate to win the dulcimer playing contests with the fiddle tunes I learned. Likewise, the music in this book has been nourished by the inspiration and support of other dulcimer players. My thanks go especially to the dulcimer players I have learned from and taught at the Appalachian State University Dulcimer Playing Workshop in Boone, NC, the Swannanoa Gathering in Asheville, NC, the Cosby Dulcimer Convention in Tennessee, Augusta Spring Dulcimer Week in West Virginia, and the other events that have kept us united.

The connection between the mountain dulcimer and traditional string band music has existed for a very long time, and is especially strong in the southwestern Virginia area. The Melton family from Galax, VA, for example, have played and built dulcimers since the 1800s and have long been known for their prowess with fiddle tunes, both in a band setting with fiddle and banjo, and in solo performance. Accounts of the early Galax conventions from the 1930s cite the great skill of the mountain dulcimer players, and even mention special presentations on its playing techniques and history.

I hope you are as happy as I am to continue the mountain dulcimer/fiddle tune traditions, and that you will enjoy this melodious, energetic music.

Lois Hornbostel

ABOUT THE AUTHOR

Over the past 20 years Lois Hornbostel has become recognized as one of the most influential mountain dulcimer players in the U.S. Her ability to play and teach many musical styles shines through in her books. Her first recording, *Vive le Dulcimer,* which contained many selections from her Mel Bay book ANTHOLOGY FOR THE FRETTED DULCIMER, was a finalist for an "INDIE" Award in the World Music Category. As accomplished in her teaching as in her musicianship, Lois has taught over 12,000 school children the basics of dulcimer playing, and is the director of the Appalachian State University Dulcimer Playing Workshop, the largest adult dulcimer "camp" in the country.

PLAYING INSTRUCTIONS

READING THE TABLATURE

Tablature is a musical notation system in which you play by fret numbers. This is illustrated below. Although standard musical notation is included for all the tunes in this book, the tablature serves a special purpose. Beyond regular notation, it is a "road map" for your fingers that will help them move efficiently and gracefully through the music. Left-hand fingerings are suggested in some selected arrangements. T = thumb. I – index. M = middle. R = ring. P = pinky.

The arrangements in this book are written for the basic 3-string mountain dulcimer. As you look down at your dulcimer, if it has two strings spaced close together that sit closest to you, they will be tuned in unison and considered as one string (your first string) in the tablature.

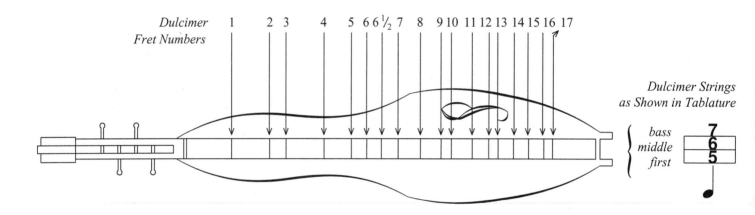

As shown in the above illustration, the three lines in the tablature indicate the three strings. The numbers above each line tell you the fret at which that string is to be played with your left-hand fingers. In the above example, that would mean the first string is pressed down just to the left of the 5th fret, the middle string, just to the left of the 6th fret; and the bass string, just to the left of the 7th fret.

In the interest of keeping the tablatures uncluttered and easy to read, two things are done that you should note:

1. O's (or open, unfretted notes) are not written in, EXCEPT where O is the melody note:

2. If a note or chord is held for more than one beat, it is written just once. Continue playing it to the rhythm indications below the tablature until the next note or chord appears.

Under the bottom line of the tablatures you will find standard tablature timing symbols. They make it easier for your eye to catch the time value for each note when playing the tablature and suggest strumming patterns. They look slightly different from regular note timings. Here's how they compare:

In addition to tablature and musical notation, accompaniment chord symbols are given above the notation. These can be played on any accompaniment instrument, such as guitar, and if you wish to use the dulcimer to back up other instruments or your voice, accompaniment chords are provided next to the tuning instructions in this book.

RIGHT - HAND TECHNIQUES *

The arrangements in this book are in chord-melody style (playing melody notes and adding chord changes as a guitar would). They are written for strumming across all the strings, as in traditional dulcimer playing. The strummed dulcimer's voice and rhythms are similar to the sounds of a fiddle being bowed in double stops with a shuffle rhythm. A fiddler usually adds many quick notes around the main melody. The arrangements in this book present the basic melodies without much ornamentation. This makes them easier to learn and more articulate on the dulcimer, and will work well if you play by yourself or want to play with a fiddle, reinforcing the basic melody line.

Workin' on a Good Strum:

Try to keep your strumming very steady. Fiddle tunes are traditionally dance music with no variation in tempo. If you are a newer player you may want to practice keeping a steady beat with your strum. One way to do this is to listen to this book's companion recording and strum along in half time, muting your strings by softly resting your left hand across the strings around the first fret. The steady beat of a metronome can also help you. Advice on playing faster will come later.

The traditional strum played on the mountain dulcimer is affectionately called the "Bump-diddly", which is similar to the fiddle bow's shuffle. It can be compared to a quarter note–two eighth notes rhythm pattern (♩ ♫). Most of the longer held notes are broken down into this strum pattern here, so if you learn the two kinds of strums you'll be able to play the arrangements in this book.

If you see below the tablature the rhythm: | , strum OUT (↗) across all the strings. This strum will be equal to a quarter note (♩), and gets one beat.

If you see below the tablature the rhythm: ⌐⌐ , quickly strum out-in (⋀ , picture an A-frame). These two quick strums are equal in time to two eighth notes (♫). They take the same amount of time as the one quarter note, or OUT strum, above.

Since most players prefer to strum the main notes of a tune out, away from them, this is being explained in their terms. If you prefer to strum most of your notes in, toward you (either preference is equally valid), you can reverse the strum directions to IN (↓) and check-mark (↙).

* Apologies to left-handed players who strum with their left hands and note with their right. Please reverse the terminologies "right" and "left" in this book.

Here's a nice little strumming exercise for strum directions, counting time, and relating strums to tablature time symbols:

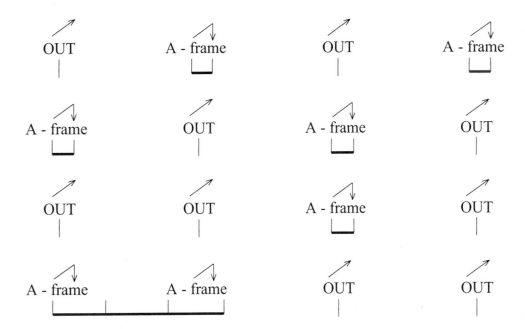

The arrangement of "Fly Around, My Pretty Little Miss" has the strum arrows written below the tablature time values to help you become accustomed to how to strum them.

Feel free to trade quarter note strums for two-eighth-note strums and digress from the strum patterns shown in the tablature arrangements. Please just count your time right.

Articulating Melody Notes When Strumming:

You can change the angle of your strum as it travels straight across your dulcimer's strings. This can help keep the melody louder than the harmony notes. When most of the notes occur on the first string, instead of moving your pick flat across all the strings, angle your strum so it moves like this:

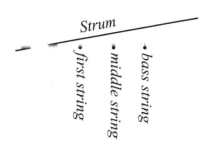

The flex action of your pick will lightly pick up the harmony notes from the other strings.

If the melody notes occur on the bass string, angle your strum like this:

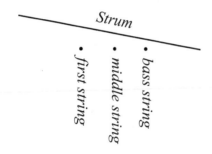

If the melody notes are on the middle string, experiment with strumming flat across all the strings, or if you hear the higher-tuned first string overpowering the middle string melody notes, try angling slightly toward the bass string.

Other Right-Hand Styles * :

You can adapt the arrangements in this book to accommodate other styles of playing. Instead of strumming you can:

1. Flatpick the arrangements by using your pick on just the melody notes individually. You can add some harmony by strumming some of the chords. Good times for strums are at the beginning and middle of a measure, or at odd times to create upbeat accents and syncopations.

2. Crosspick (with a pick) or Fingerpick (with your fingers) the arrangements, breaking down the strums into picking patterns.

3. Mountain dulcimers can also be Bowed with a fiddle or psaltery bow for a very interesting sound, and these arrangements can be played on a bowed mountain dulcimer.

Picks

Many varieties of picks can be used to strum fiddle tunes on mountain dulcimers. Here are two different styles that work well in different ways.

If you like a solid, medium-weight pick to strum your dulcimer, a good one is the Herdim pick. These became popular in the 1970s among mountain dulcimer players. They are articulate, hard to wear out, have three points of somewhat varying thickness, and have less flapping sound than most picks. They are manufactured in Germany, not found in most music stores, but the larger dealers of mountain dulcimers can usually supply them. They are rather expensive. While their thickness can produce volume well, it also can tire your arm and produce some rough string sounds when strumming fast. They also work well for flat/crosspicking.

Some players prefer a lightweight pick for strumming, but the problem here has always been the flapping sound getting in the way of the melody. A nice option here is the white nylon Jim Dunlop .46mm pick. They're more articulate than the longer light picks, although not as much so as the heavier Herdim. The Dunlop's light weight and composition give it an intriguing subtle syncopation from the bend of the pick reminiscent of historical strumming styles, and a nice lightness on the strings. They are easy on your arm. The embossed logo sometimes needs filing down to avoid catching in the strings, and they have some flapping sound. A pick this light is not usually ideal for flat/crosspicking.

*   More details on playing these styles are given in ANTHOLOGY FOR THE FRETTED DULCIMER, DULCIMER FIDDLE TUNES and THE IRISH DULCIMER.

LEFT-HAND TECHNIQUES

The arrangements in this book are in chord-melody style, combining the melody notes and harmonies from other strings that accommodate the standard chordal structure of these tunes. We use lots of open strings, but not all the time. This provides variety and portrays each tune's personality. Sometimes the melody notes are found on other strings than the first. This is done to make the fingering easier and in some cases to add personality to the music.

Suggested fingerings are provided in some selected tablatures. T = thumb. I = index. M = middle. R = ring. P = pinky.

You may want to use different fingerings from those suggested, depending on the size, shape and flexibility of your own hand, and your dulcimer's fret spacing. The tablatures with fingerings give examples of typical passages found in other tunes in this book.

Although there are volumes of left-hand techniques that can be studied, here are some that will help you with the music in this book:

1. The less motion you put into changing your fingerings around, the smoother the music will flow.

2. Articulation and tone. In most cases, the pads of your fingertips do the best job of holding the strings down. Positioning your wrist a little higher can add power to your fingering. Make solid contact with the string and the wood below. Stop the strings next to the frets (not on top of them) for the clearest tone. After you have strummed, don't immediately lift up your fingers, but let them linger just a little to draw out the tone of the note. Keep as much contact with the strings as you can. Try to slide from one hand position to another rather than lifting your fingers, changing position and putting them down again. Try to keep the tone ringing. A staccato sound is nice for variety but not for every note.

3. Efficiency of fingering. Try to "center" your fingers along the fretboard, with your index or thumb generally reaching up for higher notes and your ring or pinky reaching down for lower.

    Try "double fretting" a string to prepare for notes to come. For example, if you are playing a run of notes down the fretboard, your ring finger can be holding down the string at a lower fret while your index or thumb is playing the higher frets. When it's time to play the note your ring finger has been "reserving", just lift the upper finger and you're there. Movement is more balanced than if your fingers just hopped their way down the fretboard. Try to plan ahead this way and save yourself some work. Examples of this technique are found in "Fly Around My Pretty Little Miss" and "Julie Ann Johnson".

Slurs:

A valuable left-hand technique is playing "slurs". This is the term used when a fiddler plays two or more different notes on a single bow stroke. Although you are strumming or picking the strings of your dulcimer, your left hand will often be playing more than one note on a single strum or pick. Hammer-ons and pull-offs are the most common slurs played on the dulcimer, and they enable you to play fast sequences of notes and add lightness to the sound of your playing. Here's how to play them and how they look in tablature:

How to Play	**Tablature Example**

Hammer-On

⌒

2   3

Place your ring or middle finger at fret 2, play that note, and then immediately "hammer" down on fret 3 with your index finger. (You'll be getting two notes "for the price of one".)

(Hammer-on is indicated by a curved line above the fret numbers.)

Pull-Off

3   2

‿

Play the string while your index finger is on fret 3 and your middle finger is on fret 2, and immediately pull your index off fret 3 so the note at fret 2 sounds.

(Pull-off is indicated by a curved line below the fret numbers.)

Hammer-ons and pull-offs can be substituted with "slides". Slides are done by playing a string at one note and sliding your fretting finger up or down the fretboard to the next note.

MEMORIZING THE TUNES:

To memorize a tune it helps to listen to it over and over. This book's companion recording will help you with that. Concentrate on one tune at a time and don't try to analyze it too much at first. Play it in the background while you're driving the car, washing the dishes, etc. After a while try humming along with it. When you can hum it without the recording playing, or at least know how it should sound, look at the arrangement in the book.

Look at the rhythms below the tablature and try strumming just the rhythm as you hum the melody. Don't try to go as fast as the recording and don't try to play the melody notes yet. You can mute your strings by gently resting your left hand across them at the low end of the fretboard, below fret 1. When you have practiced the slow strumming, look at the beginning of the tablature, taking note if it starts with a pick-up before the first measure, and considering which fingers you will use. Play with both hands through the first measure or two, or the first phrase. Practice this until you can hear the tune begin to emerge from your dulcimer. Also, look at the visual path, or pattern, the tune takes as it travels up and down your fretboard, and try to memorize that.

A little more work and you'll be playing the whole A part of the tune, paying attention to the repeats and recognizing the differences between the 1st and 2nd endings if the tune has them. Learn the B part (some tunes will have additional parts) using the same steps, and you're on your way!

BUILDING SPEED:

These fiddle tunes have traditionally been played for dancing and needed to be fast enough to keep the dancers in motion and inspired. Not every dance is played at the same tempo. Typical tempo ranges among dances can be found on a metronome setting of 100 to 150, one quarter note per click. The same tempo is kept throughout the tune. Unless you are playing for dancers or with other musicians who play fast, you may like to play the tunes slower. With the exception of the waltzes, keep the tunes moving at a lively pace but don't feel you have to play them at breakneck speed. Many of these melodies are so rich they can be played at much slower tempos and take on a new beauty and interest. It's musically valid to experiment with the speed. That said, here is how you can build your speed if you want to play the tunes at dance tempos.

I recommend practicing with a metronome. First, review the tablature and find the section that is the most challenging for you, and practice that section. Next, set the metronome's click slow, so you can play the challenging section in time with it. Then try adding on the measures before and after the challenging section, and keep practicing until the phrase goes smoothly. Continue adding measures and practicing until you have the whole part of the tune steady. You're halfway home. Learn the next part the same way.

When you can play the whole tune at a slow and steady tempo with the metronome, increase the clicks 1 to 5 points. Practice at the new tempo until you are comfortable. Continue to build your speed, practicing at slow increases like this. It makes the process easier and your playing solid.

PLAYING YOUR MOUNTAIN DULCIMER IN A STRING BAND SETTING

Although you may choose to play your dulcimer solo, or with guitar back-up, with other dulcimers, or other instrumentation, you may want to play in the traditional setting of the music in this book.

The fiddle tunes here are often referred to as "old time string band" music, a traditional American style of music at the roots of country and bluegrass. The basic string band instruments are the fiddle, clawhammer banjo and guitar. The fiddle is the lead instrument, has the highest voice and is typically played the "fanciest". The banjo traditionally reinforces the core melody and plays some harmonies about an octave below the fiddle. The guitar's voice is below the banjo's, and it provides chords and bass rhythm. Many other stringed instruments, including the mountain dulcimer, play this music well and have been blended successfully with the original three instruments.

The possibilities for mountain dulcimer in this setting are varied. Here are some ways its melodic range, harmony possibilities, strong rhythms, and unique voice can contribute to the overall sound of a string band:

Melody: You can reinforce the fiddle's melody line, one or two octaves below, or in the same octave at the upper end of your fretboard. A band setting is not usually the best place for shows of virtuosity or subtle ornamentation. They will not be heard, and since the fiddle is the lead instrument you want to complement it by playing the basic melody, much the same as the banjo, which has a lot of the same melodic range as the dulcimer.

Harmony: The harmonies of typical guitar chords are built into the arrangements in this book. By playing in this chord-melody style, you are harmonizing with the fiddle's melody voice. You may choose to play straight accompaniment chords. Drones, part of the traditional sounds of the dulcimer, are the harmony of choice by fiddlers on many tunes. You can also play single-string runs on your first or bass strings and counter melodies as a banjo would to separate its voice and add color to the overall sound.

Rhythm: Strumming across three or more strings as we do presents exciting opportunities to contribute to the rhythm. Take your cues from the fiddle's phrasing. Where is it emphasizing the upbeat, the downbeat? When is the fiddler accenting loud or soft notes? Try to support and blend. Busy, fast strumming is not always the best contribution to the overall sound. Sometimes judiciously placed accent strums that work with the fiddle's voice are best.

Tone Color: Although voices vary from one dulcimer to another, there are some basic qualities they have in common. These qualities are in some ways similar, and in some ways different from the standard string band instruments.

Like the guitar, the dulcimer is played with a pick and can be used for accompaniment chords. But its voice is higher, brighter. Unlike the guitar style used in string bands, traditionally all the dulcimer's strings are strummed together, which gives it a different harmony combination and rhythm voice.

The clawhammer banjo is plucked and beaten with the fingers and has less sustain than the dulcimer. Like banjoists, dulcimer players are in the habit of using frequent hammer-ons, pull-offs and slides to play quick notes and syncopations.

The fiddle is bowed, which sets it apart from the picked instruments. It is louder and its voice cuts through the others. One bow stroke can combine several high-speed notes or sustain one long note. The bowing can be very rhythmic, even percussive. It often sounds like a human voice. The dulcimer's voice can add to the fiddle's by singing in unison with it, harmonizing with it, sharing drones, and emphasizing rhythm.

VOLUME BALANCE FOR YOUR MOUNTAIN DULCIMER:

The fiddle, banjo and guitar are each individually louder than most mountain dulcimers. Dulcimer builders in recent years have made more acoustically responsive instruments, but you may want to consider some simple amplification.

Although string bands are traditionally acoustic, not containing electronic instruments, in performances and competitions the volume balances among the instruments have long been adjusted with microphones and PA soundboards. If you are in such a situation, make sure your volume is increased so your dulcimer's voice can be heard in the blend. Aim the microphone at a soundhole, and not too near your pick. *

In less formal settings like jam sessions, many dulcimer players use small, portable amplifiers that can be placed beside or under a chair. Acoustic-sounding pick-ups can be installed in your dulcimer, or you can stick one to its top, on the soundboard.

* Beware excessive pick flap that overpowers your strummed dulcimer's voice, whether you are playing acoustically or amplified. Experiment with firmer picks or strumming at different areas along your fretboard and strum hollow.

KICK-OFFS:

Kick-offs are short musical introductions often played on a fiddle before a tune begins. When playing with other instruments kick-offs establish the tempo and get everyone started together. Here are a few good kick-offs. They are demonstrated in the most common tuning in this book, DAD. You can transpose them to the tunes in other tunings if you pay attention to the scales in those other tunings and where these kick-offs fall in those scales.

Four Potatoes: **or: "Mashed" Potatoes** (with slides):

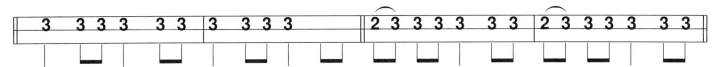

You could play the 4 Potatoes on open strings. Some other places you could fret while strumming this rhythm are at frets 2, 4 or 7 on your first or bass string.

Note: If there is a pick-up (♩ or ♫) at the start of the tune, it is played as the last beat of the kick-off.

Another good kick-off is to play the last 2 or 4 measures of the tune. The following example is the last 2 measures of "Yellow Rose of Texas:"

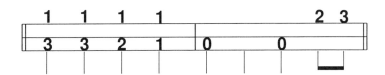

These are just a few ways of playing kick-offs. Now try to make up some of your own!

TAGS:

Tags are bits of music that finish off the tunes. Here are some good tags in DAD tuning:

A Single Harmonic:

A harmonic played on all the strings at the 7th fret is a good finish, producing a nice little chime. It is played by lightly touching, rather than pressing, the strings directly above the fret, and strumming the string once. Immediately after the strum, the finger lightly touching the strings is quickly lifted and the chime is produced. A little practice and you can do it. Harmonics are shown in the example below with hyphens on both sides of of the number.

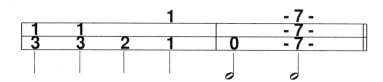

An ending harmonic like this is usually played as the last half or quarter note in the last measure of the tune.

Descending Tags: or:

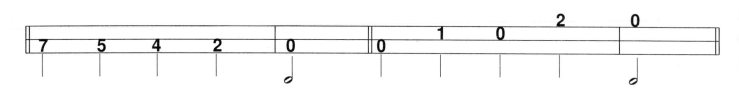

Ascending Tags: or:

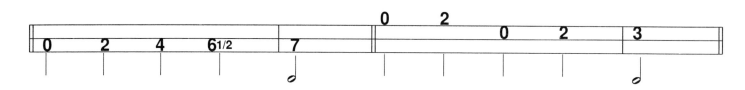

Country Chordal:

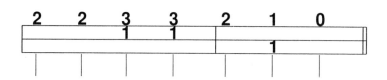

18

Shave & a Hair Cut:

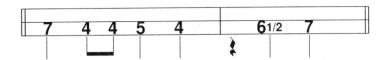

Barn Dance:

Show-off (triplets and harmonic):

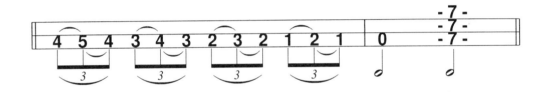

Now try making up a few tags of your own!

PERSONALIZING THE TUNES:

The arrangements presented in this book are intended to serve as models. Models and examples are powerful learning tools.

Once you have learned the tunes from this book I encourage you to personalize them. Vary the strum patterns, the accents, improvise a bit on the melody, play with the harmonies, or make other changes to suit your own musical personality.

HOW TO TUNE YOUR DULCIMER:

These tunes are arranged in the DAD tuning. Tune your dulcimer as follows:

D - first string
A - middle string
D - bass string

Tune your bass string to D below Middle C. Then fret that bass string at the 4th fret, sound that note (which will be A), and tune your middle string to it. Finally, sound the bass string at the 7th fret (which will be octave D), and tune your first string to it. This is the same note as the D string on a fiddle.

The most common way to play a D scale in this tuning is from O (open) to 7 on the first string.

Most mountain dulcimers have a "6-1/2" fret in addition to a 6th fret. This enables you to play either a Mixolydian scale (using the 6th fret, omitting 6-1/2), or a D Major scale (using the 6-1/2 fret, omitting the 6th).

ACCOMPANIMENT CHORDS:

Above the musical notations you will see accompaniment chord symbols. They can be played on your dulcimer or on other instruments, like guitars. Some favorite forms of these chords that go well with these tunes are listed below. There are many other inversions of these chords in the DAD tuning, but these are some that work especially well for accompaniment.

One of the advantages of the DAD tuning and other "octave" tunings is that you can vary the chords by inverting them. For example:

2		0
0	can become	0
0		2

D Chords

0	2	0	2	4	4	- bass string
0	0	3	3	3	5	- midd. string
0	0	0	0	0	0	- first string

D/C♯	D/B	D/A	G Chords			
2	2	2	3	3	3	5
2	1	0	1	3	3	6
0	0	0	0	3	5	0

A Chords						A7 Chords		
1	1	4	4	4	4	3	4	6 1/2
0	2	2	0	4	4	0	4	6
1	1	1	4	4	6 1/2	1	3	4

Bm Chords				Em Chords			E7 Chords	
2	2	5	5	1	3	5	1	5
1	3	5	5	1	1	4	1	6 1/2
0	5	5	7	1	1	3	0	0

C Chords

3	6	6
4	4	6
6	6	6

Fly Around, My Pretty Little Miss

Key: D
Tuning: DAD

The arrows below the tablature are explained in the strumming instructions at the beginning of this book.
They show directions to move your pick and can help you count time.

For your fretting hand, the "double fretting" technique works well at the start of this piece. Start with your
ring finger at fret 7 and leave it there while your index finger travels to frets 8, 9 and 8. Then lift up your
index and you will be ready to strum the note at fret 7 again. Your hand is not wasting motion and is balanced
on the fret board.

Examples of melody embellishments

A Part, measure 2:

A Part, measure 7:

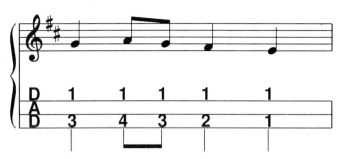

Examples of rhythm embellishments

A Part, measures 2 + 3:

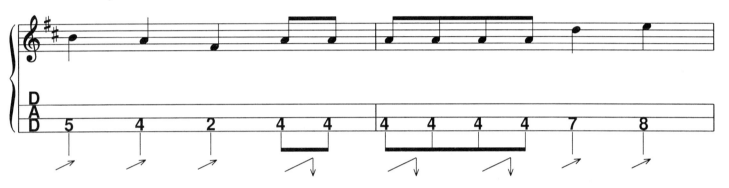

Some words to sing with the A part:

> Fly around, my pretty little miss,
> Fly around, my Daisy.
> Fly around, my pretty little miss,
> You almost drive me crazy.
>
> Wish I was in the Western Country,
> Sittin' in a chair.
> One arm round the whiskey jug,
> The other round my dear.

Bonaparte's Retreat

Key: D

Tuning: DAD

There are many different versions of this fiddler's standard, sometimes in other keys and at different tempos. This setting is probably the most familiar and is usually played at a slower, more stately, pace.

In the B part there is a "slur" from fret 1 to fret 2. A hammer-on would work fine, but the juicier sound of a slide is more like what you would hear on a fiddle.

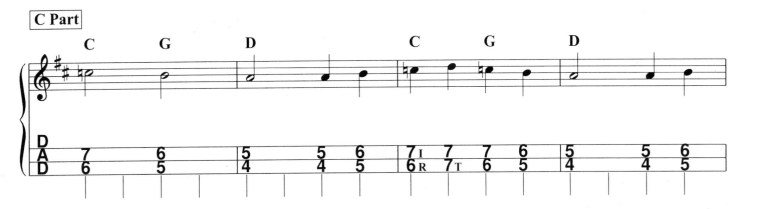

Repeat B Part

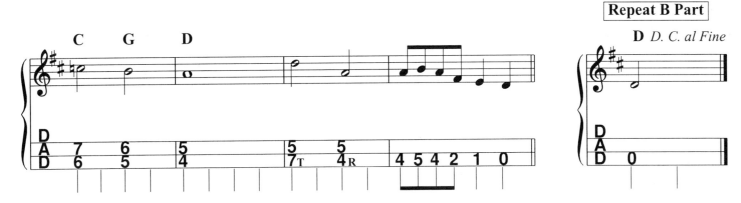

Some words to sing with this tune:

A Part: Met the girl I love
         in a town way down in Dixie.
         'Neath the stars above
         she was the sweetest girl I ever did see.

B Part: So, I took her in my arms
         and told her of her many charms.
         I kissed her as the fiddles played
         the "Bonaparte's Retreat".

C Part: All the world was bright
         as I held her on that night.
         And I heard her say,
         "Please don't go away".

B Part: She's gone and I'll admit I knew
         That I had met my Waterloo.
         I knew that we would say adieu
         To "Bonaparte's Retreat".

Bonaparte Crossing the Rhine

Key: D

Tuning: DAD

Like the previous "Bonaparte" tune, this is usually played a bit slower and more stately than most fiddle tunes, giving it the feeling of a march designed to insight valor.

*   At the end of 1st time through, play fret 1 on bass string along with pick-up notes.

The Yellow Rose of Texas

Key: D

Tuning: DAD

This is the traditional fiddle version of this tune, not the song played frequently on the radio in the 1950 s.
The following arrangement uses the lower octave on your dulcimer's fretboard. For variety you can play tunes
an octave higher, and the second tablature is an example of that. Try working out comfortable fingerings in
the second arrangement.

Same Tune an Octave Higher:

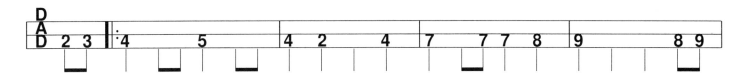

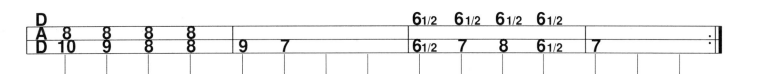

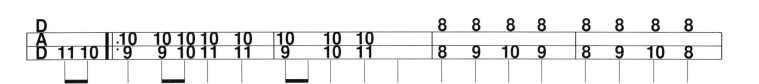

Forked Deer

Key: D

Tuning: DAD

This is arranged simply, to play the tune up to speed. The options after the arrangement duplicate what most fiddlers would play. Banjo players usually play simplified versions of notey fiddle passages like these.

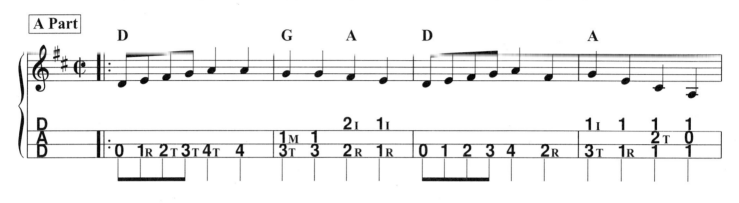

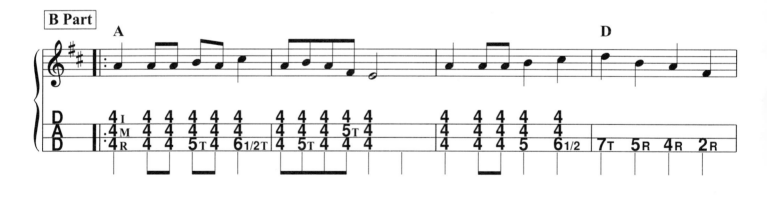

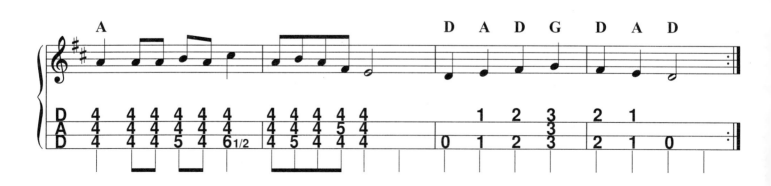

Options:

Part A, measure 4:

Part A, measure 7 + 8:

Part B, measure 4:

Julie Ann Johnson

Key: D

Tuning: DAD

Your fretting hand will move easier if you "double fret" the first string when you begin. Start by putting your thumb at fret 9 and your ring finger at fret 5 (same string). Leave your ring finger down as your thumb plays frets 9, 8 and 7, then lift and strum the note at fret 5. This will balance your hand on the fretboard and help you articulate the notes.

It is fun to improvise a little on the melody of a fiddle tune. This is done in the variations listed after the tablature. Try composing some of your own variations.

32

Variations

Part B, measures 5 + 6:

Chinese Breakdown

Key: D

Tuning: DAD

This tune is reminiscent of cartoon music, and it's lots of fun to play. It makes a good contest tune. Don't race through it, but play with dynamics (louds and softs) and try adding variations to the melody.

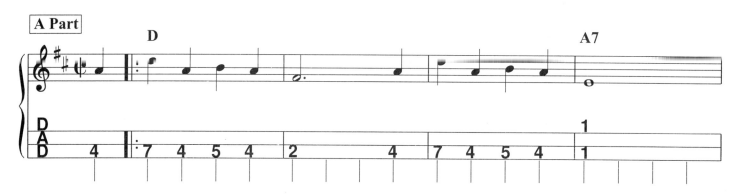

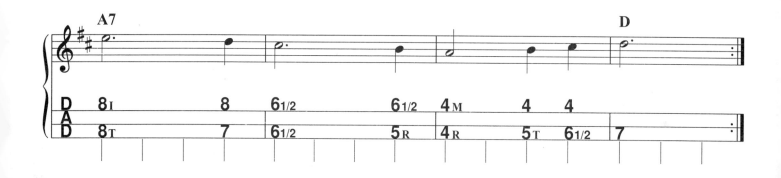

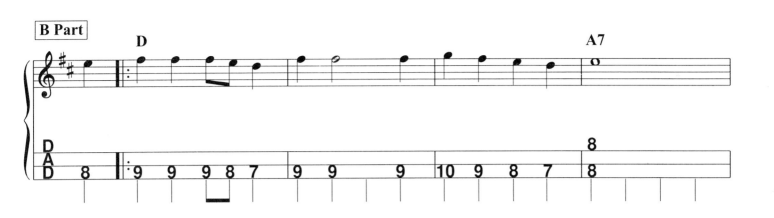

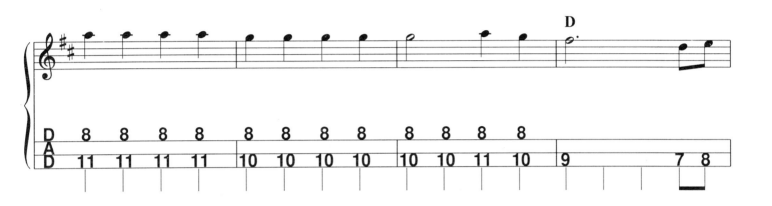

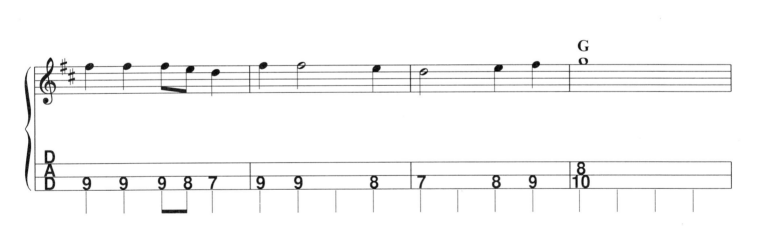

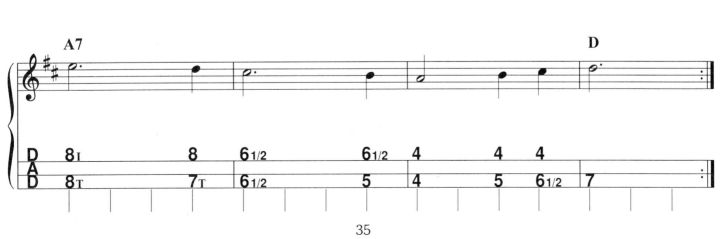

35

Rock the Cradle, Joe

Key: D
Tuning: DAD

Fiddlers often add syncopation to the straight rhythms of a tune. In the B part, the second and sixth measures have typical syncopations. It will help you hear the syncopations if you clap them out before you play.

Sugar Hill

Key: D
Tuning: DAD

This tune is a favorite around Galax, Virginia. The beginning of this arrangement shows a 3-note slur on one strum, which starts the tune with an authentic fiddle sound. To accomplish it, give your dulcimer a strong strum, angled toward the bass string. Hammer-on the middle string at fret 1, then 2 and slide into fret 3. That puts you into the first measure with a little syncopation. It takes practice to get it right. If you prefer to try something simpler than the slur, just note the 4th fret on the bass string and strum a quarter note. Strum all the first measure.

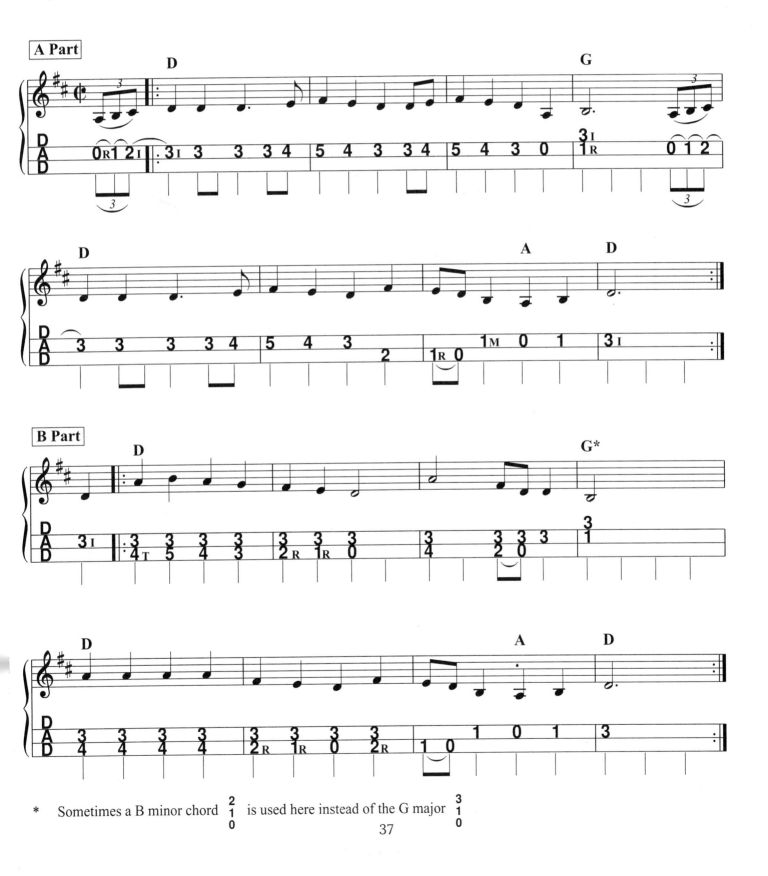

*   Sometimes a B minor chord $\begin{smallmatrix}2\\1\\0\end{smallmatrix}$ is used here instead of the G major $\begin{smallmatrix}3\\1\\0\end{smallmatrix}$

"Sugar Hill" sounds like it was a good place to stay away from. Here are some words that you can sing to the A part:

> If you wanna get your eye knocked out,
> If you wanna drink your fill.
> If you wanna get your head cut off,
> Go to Sugar Hill.
>
> I'm gettin' lonesome for my gal,
> I want a drink of rye.
> Goin' up on Sugar Hill,
> Know the reason why.
>
> Drag your banjo off the wall,
> Grab your fiddle, Bill.
> Hitch the horses to the sleigh,
> We're goin' up Sugar Hill.

"Dulcimer Enchantment." Photo by James Walkingstick.

39

Dixie

Key: D
Tuning: DAD

Before it became an anthem for the Confederacy, "Dixie" was written by Daniel Emmett as a minstrel show song. Many of the old-time fiddle tunes currently played came from minstrel shows.

"Dixie" travels up and down the scale quickly. To economize motion of your fretting hand, many of the notes are played here on the middle string.

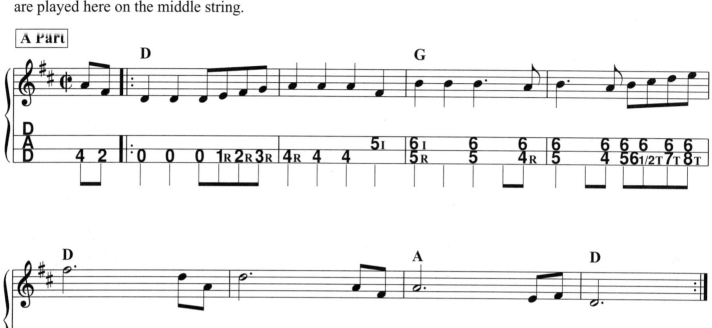

C Part

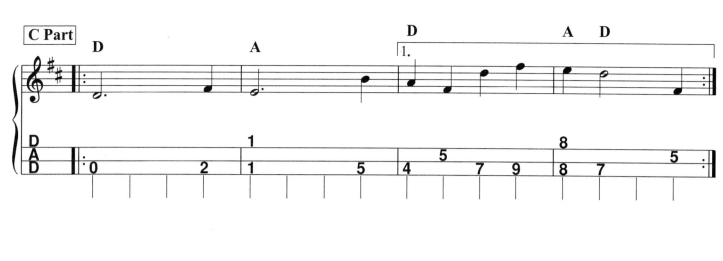

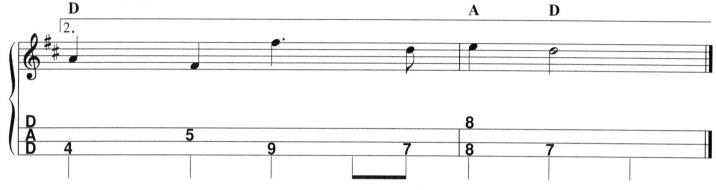

Year of Jubilo

Key: D

Tuning: DAD

Fingering advice: In the second measure after you have noted fret 4 and your thumb travels to fret 9, drop your ring finger at fret 5 to prepare for the end of the measure. This "double fretting" will also balance your hand on the fretboard.

Down Yonder

Key: D
Tuning: DAD

Before playing the C part, clap out the syncopated rhythms.

Repeat A part and one time through B part, then play:

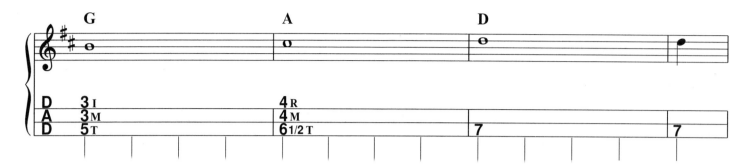

The last time through, end with it this way:

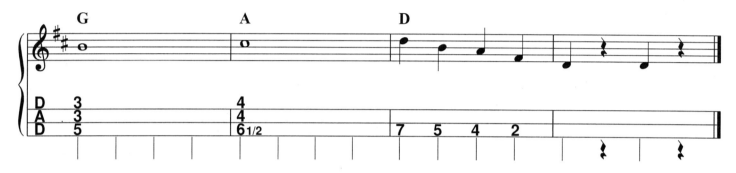

Dubuque

Key: D

Tuning: DAD

Before playing the B part, clap out the syncopated rhythms.

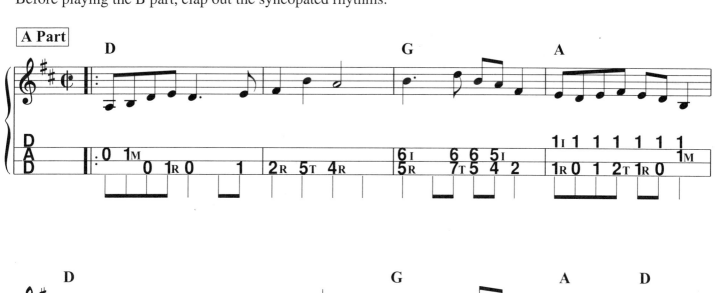

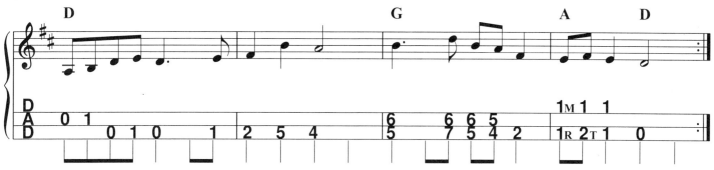

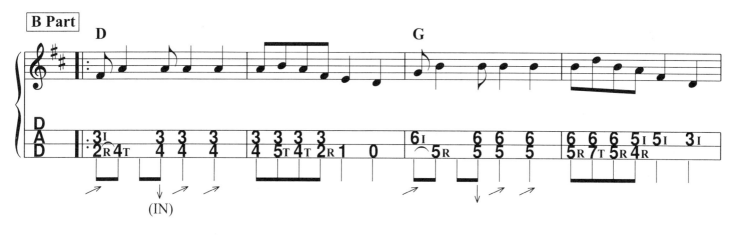

Spotted Pony

Key: D

Tuning: DAD

The B part starts with a slur into the first measure. This is similar to the start of "Sugar Hill". If you need to, check the instructions for that tune.

Variation

Part B, measures 4 + 5:

Single Footin' Horse

Key: D

Tuning: DAD

This is fun to play in a medley with "Spotted Pony" or "Dubuque".

Midnight on the Water

Key: D
Tuning: DAD

There have been many different settings of this waltz, which comes from Texas fiddler Luke Thomasson. Most fiddlers are in the habit of playing the B part twice, which comes out to 32 measures instead of the typical 16 measures for a fiddle tune part. The variation after the tablature gives a nice walking bass line, a popular device for waltzes.

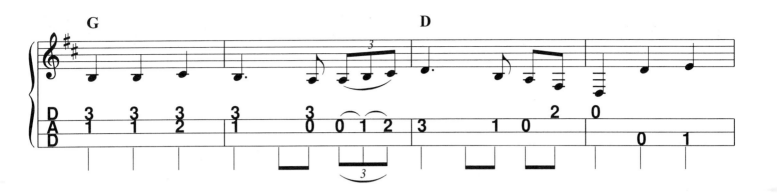

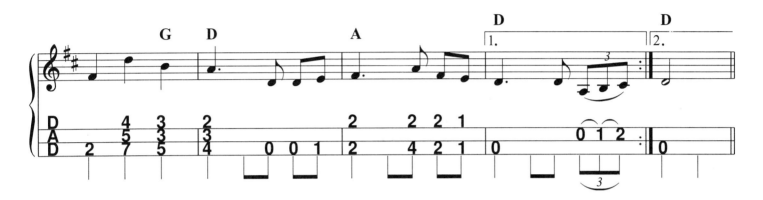

Variation

Part A, measures 1 through 4:

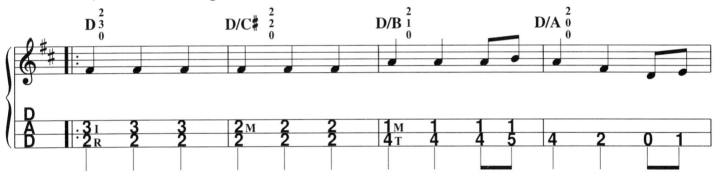

THE GDG CAPO'D TUNING:

Using a dulcimer capo can quickly change your dulcimer's key. C-clamp shaped capos designed for mountain dulcimers are sold by many dulcimer dealers. A good source and instructions for an interim capo are given below.

To get to the GDG capo'd tuning simply start with the DAD tuning described earlier, at the beginning of the D tunes. Place your capo to the left of the 3rd fret. Adjust and tighten it so the strings do not buzz and the notes ring clear. Some dulcimers may require a little re-tuning.

The 3rd fret becomes "0" or the open string. From there on, the fret numbers remain the same as in DAD tuning.* The basic scale on your first string is from 0 to 10, omitting the 9-1/2 fret.

IF YOU DON'T HAVE A CAPO:

Until you get one you can use a chopstick or other flat stick and a thick rubber band. Fasten the rubber band to one end of the stick. Place the stick to the left of the 3rd fret. Gently wrap the rubber band underneath the dulcimer and around the other end of the stick. Adjust or tighten the rubber band to avoid string buzzes. A good source for dulcimer capos is Ron Ewing Dulcimers, 224 East Maynard, Columbus, OH 43202

ACCOMPANIMENT CHORDS:

As in the earlier DAD tuning, this is an "octave" tuning, which gives you the option of inverting the following chords:

G Chords

0	5	0	5	7	- bass string
0	0	6	6	6	- middle string
0	0	0	0	5	- first string

C Chords

6	6	6	8
4	4	6	6
0	6	6	6

A Chord

4
4
4

D Chords

4	4	7	7	7
0	5	5	0	7
4	4	4	7	7

Em Chords

5	8	8
4	6	8
0	5	8

---

* Tablatures for chromatically fretted instruments, like guitars, usually re-number the frets from the capo on up the fingerboard. Since the mountain dulcimer's fret pattern is diatonic, and uneven in appearance, re-numbering all the frets would be awkward to relate to. Keeping the same number names for the frets throughout all the tunings is standard practice in writing mountain dulcimer music.

Sail Away, Ladies

Key: G

Tuning: DAD, capo 3rd fret (GDG)

This tune comes from a song made famous in the early days of the Grand Old Opry by Uncle Dave Macon.

The song is traditionally sung with this structure:

. Play one B part.

. Sing and play one A part.

. Play 2 measures of the B part, then sing this phrase 3 times, to the rest of the B part:

"Don't she rock 'em di-dee-o."

. Continue through the rest of the verses and end with one B part.

Additional verses:

Children don't you sit and cry,

Sail away, ladies, sail away.

You're gonna be angels by and by,

Sail away, ladies, sail away.

(Repeat B part chorus)

Come along, girls, and go with me, ...

we'll go back to Tennessee.   .....

(Chorus)

Just got a letter from Shiloh town, ...

Big St. Louie is burnin' down. .....

(Chorus)

Dutch Girl

Key: G

Tuning: DAD, capo 3rd fret (GDG)

This is an example of how lovely fiddle tunes can be. When you play it, make a point of avoiding the 6-1/2 fret.

53

Southern Aristocracy

Key: G

Tuning: DAD, capo 3rd fret (GDG)

The ragtime feeling of this tune comes from origins in minstrel shows.

Magpie

Key: G

Tuning: DAD, capo 3rd fret (GDG)

Arranged by Jeff Furman.
Used by permission.

This arrangement is from banjo and mountain dulcimer player Jeff Furman of Chapel Hill, North Carolina. It is flatpicked. Notice that open strummed notes are written into this tablature. Let your pick play only the strings with tablature numbers on them. If you prefer, you can also strum this arrangement.

THE DGD (OPEN) TUNING:

Tune your dulcimer as follows:

 D - first string
G - middle string
D - bass string

As in the DAD tuning, you tune your bass string to D below Middle C. Then fret that bass string at the 3rd fret, sound that note (which will be G), and tune your middle string to it. Finally sound the bass string at the 7th fret (octave D), and tune your first string to it.

The most common way to play a scale in this tuning is from 3 to 10 on the first string, omitting the 6-1/2 fret.

ACCOMPANIMENT CHORDS:

In the DGD tuning we have another "octave" tuning, which gives you the option of inverting the following chords:

G Chords

3	3	5	5
0	2	0	4
0	0	3	3

C Chords

3	3	3	8
3	3	3	7
1	3	6	6

D Chords

0	2	0	2	4
1	1	4	4	4
0	0	0	0	2

D7 Chords

2	4	4
3	3	4
0	0	6

Em Chords

1	3	3	5
2	2	5	5
1	1	5	5

Bm Chords

2	2
2	4
0	5

Barlow Knife

Key: G

Tuning: DGD

Start the first measure by double fretting your ring finger at fret 2 and your thumb at fret 3. This will prepare you for the lower note when you get to the end of the measure. Using the thumb is whole-heartedly recommended when it helps you reach the notes without straining your hand in difficult positions that slow you down. In the C part it helps you "walk" easily around the middle string, so the music flows smoothly.

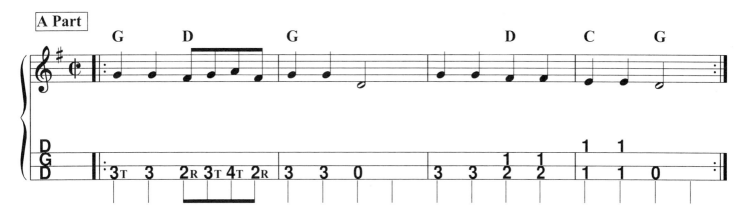

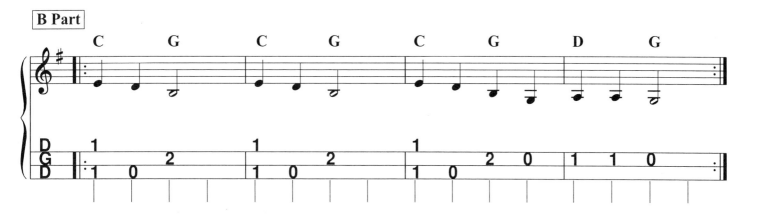

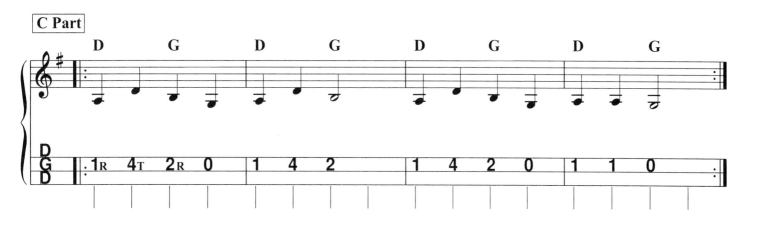

Turkey in the Straw

Key: G
Tuning: DGD

Some of the rhythms in the B part are like those in "Dubuque". This is a well-known tune, but not necessarily easy to play. The first tablature presents most of the notes a fiddler would play. The second presents the core melody and can be played faster.

High Speed Simplification:

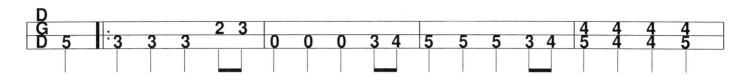

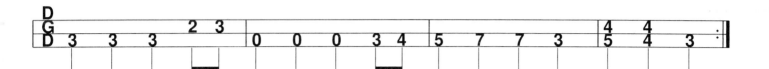

Tombigbee River

Key: G

Tuning: DGD

Midwestern fiddler Dan Gellert does a great rendition of this traditional waltz/song.

* These measures are stretched out into two measures
  when singing, as follows:

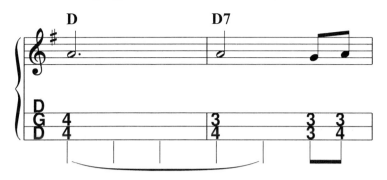

TOMBIGBEE RIVER

On the Tombigbee River so bright, I was born
In a hut made of husks of the tall yellow corn.
Was there that I met with my Jula so true,
And I rowed her around in my gumtree canoe.

Chorus : Sing, roll away, roll, on the waters so blue,
                 Like a feather we'll float in my gumtree canoe.

All day in the fields of soft cotton I'd hoe,
Think of my Jula and sing as I go.
I'd catch her a little bird with a wing of true blue,
And at night row her 'round in my gumtree canoe.

(Repeat Chorus)

With my hand on my banjo and my toe on the oar,
I'll sing her a song to the river's soft roar.
While the bright stars look down on my Jula so true,
And they dance in her eyes in my gumtree canoe.

(Chorus)

One day the old river took us so far away,
That we couldn't go back, so I thought I'd just stay.
We spied a tall ship with a flag of true blue,
And she took us in tow in my gumtree canoe.

(Chorus)

Westphalia Waltz

Key: G

Tuning: DGD

With the exception of "Cluck Old Hen" the tunes in this section are all played in the EAA tuning. There are other A tunings for the mountain dulcimer, but the EAA tuning is exciting for fiddle tunes because it has strong similarities to the AEAE tuning used by many fiddlers. The harmonies and open drones in both tunings sound alike, and the spacings of the notes along the dulcimer's fretboard duplicate many of the fingerings a fiddler uses in AEAE. Our EAA tuning also gives us the option of playing both A Major or A modal tunes.

HOW TO TUNE YOUR DULCIMER:

Tune your dulcimer as follows:

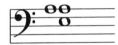 A - first and middle strings
D - bass string

Tune your bass string to E below Middle C. Then fret that bass string at the 3rd fret, sound that note (which will be A), and tune your middle and first strings to it.

The most common way to play the A scale in this tuning is from O (open) to 7 on the first string. The Major scale uses the 6-1/2 fret, omitting the 6th fret. The Mixolydian scale uses the 6th fret, omitting the 6-1/2 fret.

ACCOMPANIMENT CHORDS:

A Chords

0	0	3	5	5
0	0	0	0	4
0	2	4	7	7

D Chords / **E Chords**

1	3	3	6	0	2	0	4	4
0	3	3	5	1	1	4	4	4
3	3	5	7	1	1	4	4	6 1/2

F♯m Chords / **Bm Chords**

1	3	5	1	1	4
0	2	5	1	1	3
2	5	5	1	3	5

64

Cotton-Eyed Joe

Key: A
Tuning: EAA

Lots of fiddlers play drones on their fiddles, just like on mountain dulcimers. At the start of the B part, try sliding from fret 2 to fret 3 on the bass string.

A Part   A + E drones.

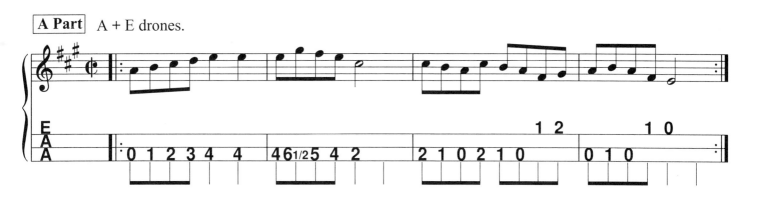

B Part

Don't you remember long time ago,
Daddy worked a man named Cotton-Eyed Joe.

Chorus: Where did you come from, where did you go?
Where did you come from, Cotton-Eyed Joe?

Wanna go to meetin' but I didn't get to go,
'Cause I had to stay home with Cotton-Eyed Joe.

(Repeat chorus)

Tune up the fiddle and rosin up the bow,
Play a little tune called "Cotton-Eyed Joe".

(Chorus)

Breakin' up Christmas

Key: A
Tuning: EAA

When you strum this tune, accent the backbeat (up beat). The first line of the tablature shows accent marks where the backbeats are. Vary this accent so the music has rhythmic variety. Sometimes this tune is started with what we're calling the B part here. Sometimes in fiddle tunes single phrases, rather than lyrics, are sung. You can sing the following to the A part:

Santa Claus done come and gone,
Breakin' up Christmas right along.

66

Variation: play this line 4 times to replace the A part.

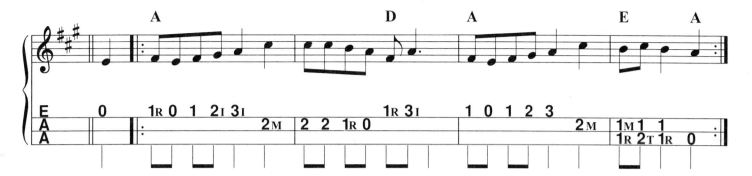

Boatmen

Key: A

Tuning: EAA

*   Sometimes an F♯m chord $\begin{smallmatrix}1\\0\\2\end{smallmatrix}$ is used here instead of the D major $\begin{smallmatrix}1\\0\\3\end{smallmatrix}$.

Sandy Boys

Key: A

Tuning: EAA

This is an interesting modal (Mixolydian) tune played by a lot of old-time fiddlers. At the start of the B part you can play an interesting slur by sliding from fret 2 up to fret 4.

John Brown's Dream

Key: A
Tuning: EAA

If you're ever around Galax, Virginia, looking to meet musicians, just park yourself on a street corner and play this tune. At the start of the B part, try sliding up to the 4th fret from the 3rd fret.

Lois Hornbostel.

Hangman's Reel

Key: A
Tuning: EAA

I have heard this 4-part tune played many times at fiddle conventions in the Southeast. Banjo players like this as much as the fiddlers. This arrangement uses hammer-ons and pull-offs like some of those played typically on clawhammer banjo. At the start of the C part, try struming open and hammering-on to the chord at fret 1. This is one way to add dynamics and variety to long tunes like this one. Strum harder when accent marks are shown.

D Part

Little Billy Wilson

Key: A
Tuning: EAA

Another pretty tune. The C part uses some interesting chords that add texture and invite different dynamics in the strumming.

Cluck Old Hen

Key: A Modal (Dorian)
Tuning: DAD

By playing melody on the two outside strings together in the DAD tuning, we have the open A string ringing out. That, along with the notes we play, puts us in A Dorian. Avoid the 6-1/2 fret. This presents a good opportunity to play "Cluck Old Hen" in a medley with a D major tune played in DAD tuning.

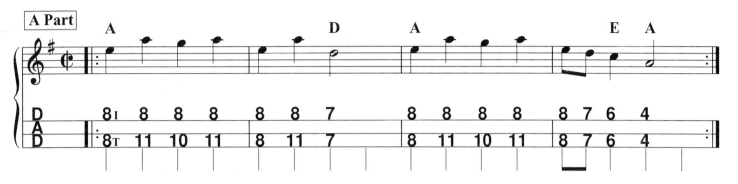

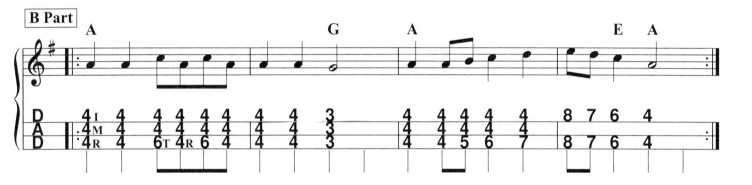

High-speed simplification:

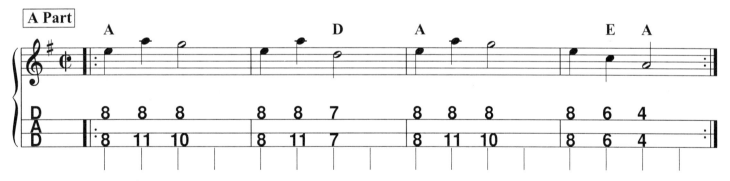

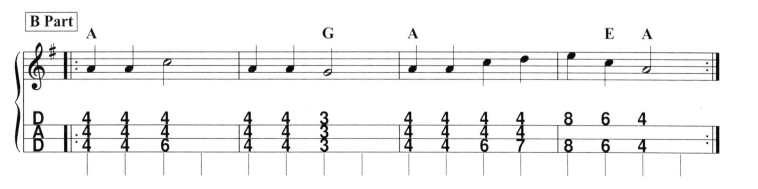

Some lyrics:

My old hen's a good old hen,
She lays eggs for the railroad men.
Sometimes one, sometimes two,
Sometimes enough for the whole darn crew.

Chorus:　Cluck old hen, cluck and sing,
Ain't laid an egg since way last Spring.
Cluck old hen, cluck and squall,
Ain't laid an egg since way last Fall.

My old hen, she cackles a lot,
Next time she cackles, she cackles in the pot!
My old hen she won't do,
She lays eggs and taters too.

(Repeat chorus)

Great Music at Your Fingertips